First published in Great Britain in 1994
by William Heinemann Ltd
an imprint of Reed Children's Books
Michelin House, 81 Fulham Road, London SW3 6RB
and Auckland, Melbourne, Singapore and Toronto
Text copyright © 1994 Reed International Books Limited
Illustrations by Arkadia copyright © 1994 Reed International Books Limited
Based on the original television designs by Ivor Wood
copyright © 1994 Woodland Animations Ltd
ISBN 0 434 96708 4
A CIP catalogue record for this book is available at the British Library.
Printed in Great Britain by BPC Paulton Books Limited

Postman Pat's

HEINEMANN · LONDON

Aa

Postman Pat reads the address on every letter.

Miss Hubbard rides her bicycle.

Bb

Cc

Dorothy Thompson gives Pat a cabbage.

Dr Gilbertson is the village doctor.

Dd

Ee

Pat watches the eggs hatch.

Peter Fogg finds a frog.

Ff

Gg

Who forgot to shut the gate?

Jess meets a hedgehog.

Hh

Ii

Ink is messy.

Miss Hubbard makes raspberry jam.

Jj

Kk

Jess keeps away from the dog's kennel.

Pat picks up lots of letters.

Ll

Mm

A magpie has stolen Pat's keys.

Ted Glen has found a birds' nest.

Nn

Oo

Sam Waldron juggles oranges.

Pat delivers a pink parcel.

Pp

Qq

Granny Dryden makes a patchwork quilt.

Reverend Timms grows red roses.

Rr

Ss

Ted Glen buys stamps at the Post Office.

The train goes over the bridge.

Tt

Uu

Pat carries an umbrella when it rains.

Pat looks after his van.

Vv

Ww
Xx

In **winter** everyone **wears extra** clothing.

Pat has yellow pyjamas and a duvet with zigzag stripes.

Goodnight, Pat. Sleep well.

zzzz

Yy

Zz